Travel phrasebooks colle
«Everything Will Be Oka

PHRASEBOOK

— HINDI —

By Andrey Taranov

THE MOST IMPORTANT PHRASES

This phrasebook contains
the most important
phrases and questions
for basic communication
Everything you need
to survive overseas

T&P BOOKS

Phrasebook + 250-word dictionary

English-Hindi phrasebook & mini dictionary

By Andrey Taranov

The collection of "Everything Will Be Okay" travel phrasebooks published by T&P Books is designed for people traveling abroad for tourism and business. The phrasebooks contain what matters most - the essentials for basic communication. This is an indispensable set of phrases to "survive" while abroad.

You'll also find a mini dictionary with 250 useful words required for everyday communication - the names of months and days of the week, measurements, family members, and more.

T&P Books Publishing
www.tpbooks.com

ISBN: 978-1-78616-743-9

This book is also available in E-book formats.
Please visit www.tpbooks.com or the major online bookstores.

FOREWORD

The collection of "Everything Will Be Okay" travel phrasebooks published by T&P Books is designed for people traveling abroad for tourism and business. The phrasebooks contain what matters most - the essentials for basic communication. This is an indispensable set of phrases to "survive" while abroad.

This phrasebook will help you in most cases where you need to ask something, get directions, find out how much something costs, etc. It can also resolve difficult communication situations where gestures just won't help.

This book contains a lot of phrases that have been grouped according to the most relevant topics. You'll also find a mini dictionary with useful words - numbers, time, calendar, colors...

Take "Everything Will Be Okay" phrasebook with you on the road and you'll have an irreplaceable traveling companion who will help you find your way out of any situation and teach you to not fear speaking with foreigners.

TABLE OF CONTENTS

T&P Books Publishing

PRONUNCIATION

Letter	Hindi example	T&P phonetic alphabet	English example

Vowels

अ	अक्सर	[a]; [ɑ], [ə]	park; teacher
आ	आगमन	[a:]	calf, palm
इ	इनाम	[i]	shorter than in feet
ई	ईश्वर	[i], [i:]	feet, Peter
उ	उठना	[ʊ]	good, booklet
ऊ	ऊपर	[u:]	pool, room
ऋ	ऋग्वेद	[r, rⁱ]	green
ए	एकता	[e:]	longer than in bell
ऐ	ऐनक	[aɪ]	time, white
ओ	ओला	[o:]	fall, bomb
औ	औरत	[au]	loud, powder
अं	अंजीर	[ŋ]	English, ring
अः	अ से अः	[h]	home, have
ऑ	ऑफिस	[o]	cotton, pocket

Consonants

क	कमरा	[k]	clock, kiss
ख	खिड़की	[kh]	work hard
ग	गरज	[g]	game, gold
घ	घर	[gh]	g aspirated
ङ	डाकू	[ŋ]	English, ring
च	चक्कर	[tʃ]	church, French
छ	छात्र	[tʃh]	hitchhiker
ज	जाना	[dʒ]	joke, general
झ	झलक	[dʒ]	joke, general
ञ	विज्ञान	[ɲ]	canyon, new
ट	मटर	[t]	tourist, trip
ठ	ठेका	[th]	don't have
ड	डंडा	[d]	day, doctor
ढ	ढलान	[d]	day, doctor
ण	क्षण	[n]	retroflex nasal
त	ताकत	[t]	tourist, trip

Letter	Hindi example	T&P phonetic alphabet	English example
थ	थकना	[th]	don't have
द	दरवाज़ा	[d]	day, doctor
ध	धोना	[d]	day, doctor
न	नाई	[n]	sang, thing
प	पिता	[p]	pencil, private
फ	फल	[f]	face, food
ब	बच्चा	[b]	baby, book
भ	भाई	[b]	baby, book
म	माता	[m]	magic, milk
य	याद	[j]	yes, New York
र	रीछ	[r]	rice, radio
ल	लाल	[l]	lace, people
व	वचन	[v]	very, river
श	शिक्षक	[ʃ]	machine, shark
ष	भाषा	[ʃ]	machine, shark
स	सोना	[s]	city, boss
ह	हज़ार	[h]	home, have

Additional consonants

क़	क़लम	[q]	king, club
ख़	ख़बर	[h]	huge, hat
ड़	लड़का	[r]	rice, radio
ढ़	पढ़ना	[r]	rice, radio
ग़	ग़लती	[ɣ]	between [g] and [h]
ज़	ज़िन्दगी	[z]	zebra, please
झ़	टेंझर	[ʒ]	forge, pleasure
फ़	फ़ौज	[f]	face, food

LIST OF ABBREVIATIONS

English abbreviations

ab.	-	about
adj	-	adjective
adv	-	adverb
anim.	-	animate
as adj	-	attributive noun used as adjective
e.g.	-	for example
etc.	-	et cetera
fam.	-	familiar
fem.	-	feminine
form.	-	formal
inanim.	-	inanimate
masc.	-	masculine
math	-	mathematics
mil.	-	military
n	-	noun
pl	-	plural
pron.	-	pronoun
sb	-	somebody
sing.	-	singular
sth	-	something
v aux	-	auxiliary verb
vi	-	intransitive verb
vi, vt	-	intransitive, transitive verb
vt	-	transitive verb

Hindi abbreviations

f	-	feminine noun
f pl	-	feminine plural
m	-	masculine noun
m pl	-	masculine plural

HINDI
PHRASEBOOK

This section contains
important phrases that may
come in handy in various
real-life situations.
The phrasebook will help
you ask for directions, clarify
a price, buy tickets, and
order food at a restaurant

T&P Books Publishing

PHRASEBOOK
CONTENTS

T&P Books Publishing

The bare minimum

Excuse me, ...
माफ़ कीजिएगा, ...
māf kījiega, ...

Hello.
नमस्कार।
namaskār.

Thank you.
शुक्रिया।
shukriya.

Good bye.
अलविदा।
alavida.

Yes.
हाँ।
hān.

No.
नहीं।
nahin.

I don't know.
मुझे नहीं मालूम।
mujhe nahin mālūm.

Where? | Where to? | When?
कहाँ? | कहाँ जाना है? | कब?
kahān? | kahān jāna hai? | kab?

I need ...
मुझे ... चाहिए।
mujhe ... chāhie.

I want ...
मैं ... चाहता /चाहती/ हूँ।
main ... chāhata /chāhatī/ hūn.

Do you have ...?
क्या आपके पास ... है?
kya āpake pās ... hai?

Is there a ... here?
क्या यहाँ ... है?
kya yahān ... hai?

May I ...?
क्या मैं ... सकता /सकती/ हूँ?
kya main ... sakata /sakatī/ hūn?

..., please (polite request)
..., कृपया।
..., kṛpaya.

I'm looking for ...
मैं ... ढूँढ रहा /रही/ हूँ।
main ... dhūnṛh raha /rahī/ hūn.

restroom
शौचालय
shauchālay

ATM
एटीएम
eṭīem

pharmacy (drugstore)
दवा की दुकान
dava kī dukān

hospital
अस्पताल
aspatāl

police station
पुलिस थाना
pulis thāna

subway
मेट्रो
metro

taxi	टैक्सी taiksī
train station	ट्रेन स्टेशन tren steshan

My name is ...	मेरा नाम ... है। mera nām ... hai
What's your name?	आपका क्या नाम है? āpaka kya nām hai?
Could you please help me?	क्या आप मेरी मदद कर सकते /सकती/ हैं? kya āp merī madad kar sakate /sakatī/ hain?
I've got a problem.	मुझे एक परेशानी है। mujhe ek pareshānī hai.
I don't feel well.	मेरी तबियत ठीक नहीं है। merī tabiyat thīk nahin hai.
Call an ambulance!	एम्बुलेन्स बुलाओ! embulens bulao!
May I make a call?	क्या मैं एक फ़ोन कर सकता /सकती/ हूँ? kya main ek fon kar sakata /sakatī/ hūn?

I'm sorry.	मुझे माफ़ करना। mujhe māf kar do.
You're welcome.	आपका स्वागत है। āpaka svāgat hai.

I, me	मैं main
you (inform.)	तू tū
he	वह vah
she	वह vah
they (masc.)	वे ve
they (fem.)	वे ve
we	हम ham
you (pl)	तुम tum
you (sg, form.)	आप āp

ENTRANCE	प्रवेश pravesh
EXIT	निकास nikās

OUT OF ORDER	ख़राब है kharāb hai
CLOSED	बंद band
OPEN	खुला khula
FOR WOMEN	महिलाओं के लिए mahilaon ke lie
FOR MEN	पुरूषों के लिए purūshon ke lie

Questions

Where?	कहाँ?
	kahān?
Where to?	कहाँ जाना है?
	kahān jāna hai?
Where from?	कहाँ से?
	kahān se?
Why?	क्यों?
	kyon?
For what reason?	किस वजह से?
	kis vajah se?
When?	कब?
	kab?

How long?	कितना समय लगेगा?
	kitana samay lagega?
At what time?	कितने बजे?
	kitane baje?
How much?	कितना?
	kitana?
Do you have ...?	क्या आपके पास ... है?
	kya āpake pās ... hai?
Where is ...?	... कहाँ है?
	... kahān hai?

What time is it?	क्या बजा है?
	kya baja hai?
May I make a call?	क्या मैं एक फ़ोन कर सकता /सकती/ हूँ?
	kya main ek fon kar sakata /sakatī/ hūn?
Who's there?	कौन है?
	kaun hai?
Can I smoke here?	क्या मैं यहाँ सिगरेट पी सकता /सकती/ हूँ?
	kya main yahān sigaret pī sakata /sakatī/ hūn?
May I ...?	क्या मैं ... सकता /सकती/ हूँ?
	kya main ... sakata /sakatī/ hūn?

Needs

I'd like …	मुझे … चाहिए। mujhe … chāhie.
I don't want …	मुझे … नहीं चाहिए। mujhe … nahin chāhie.
I'm thirsty.	मुझे प्यास लगी है। mujhe pyās lagī hai.
I want to sleep.	मैं सोना चाहता /चाहती/ हूँ। main sona chāhata /chāhatī/ hūn.
I want …	मैं … चाहता /चाहती/ हूँ। main … chāhata /chāhatī/ hūn.
to wash up	हाथ-मुँह धोना hāth-munh dhona
to brush my teeth	दाँत ब्रश करना dānt brash karana
to rest a while	कुछ समय आराम करना kuchh samay ārām karana
to change my clothes	कपड़े बदलना kapare badalana
to go back to the hotel	होटल वापस जाना hotal vāpas jāna
to buy …	… खरीदना … kharīdana
to go to …	… जाना … jāna
to visit …	… जाना … jāna
to meet with …	… से मिलने जाना … se milane jāna
to make a call	फ़ोन करना fon karana
I'm tired.	मैं थक गया /गई/ हूँ। main thak gaya /gaī/ hūn.
We are tired.	हम थक गए हैं। ham thak gae hain.
I'm cold.	मुझे सर्दी लग रही है। mujhe sardī lag rahī hai.
I'm hot.	मुझे गर्मी लग रही है। mujhe garmī lag rahī hai.
I'm OK.	मैं ठीक हूँ। main thīk hūn.

I need to make a call.	मुझे फ़ोन करना है। mujhe fon karana hai.
I need to go to the restroom.	मुझे शौचालय जाना है। mujhe shauchālay jāna hai.
I have to go.	मुझे जाना है। mujhe jāna hoga.
I have to go now.	मुझे अब जाना होगा। mujhe ab jāna hoga.

Asking for directions

Excuse me, ...

माफ़ कीजिएगा, ...
māf kījiega, ...

Where is ...?

... कहाँ है?
... kahān hai?

Which way is ...?

... कहाँ पड़ेगा?
... kahān parega?

Could you help me, please?

क्या आप मेरी मदद करेंगे
/करेंगी/, प्लीज़?
kya āp merī madad karenge
/karengī/, plīz?

I'm looking for ...

मैं ... ढूंढ रहा /रही/ हूँ
main ... dhūnrh raha /rahī/ hūn.

I'm looking for the exit.

मैं बाहर निकलने का रास्ता
ढूंढ रहा /रही/ हूँ
main bāhar nikalāne ka rāsta
dhūnrh raha /rahī/ hūn.

I'm going to ...

मैं ... जा रहा /रही/ हूँ
main ... ja raha /rahī/ hūn.

Am I going the right way to ...?

क्या मैं ...जाने के लिए सही
रास्ते पर हूँ?
kya main ... jāne ke lie sahī
rāste par hūn?

Is it far?

क्या वह दूर है?
kya vah dūr hai?

Can I get there on foot?

क्या मैं वहाँ पैदल जा सकता
/सकती/ हूँ?
kya main vahān paidal ja sakata
/sakatī/ hūn?

Can you show me on the map?

क्या आप मुझे नक्शे पर दिखा
सकते /सकती/ हैं?
kya āp mujhe nakshe par dikha
sakate /sakatī/ hain?

Show me where we are right now.

मुझे दिखाईये कि हम इस वक्त
कहाँ हैं।
mujhe dikhaīye ki ham is vakt
kahān hain.

Here

यहाँ
yahān

There

वहाँ
vahān

This way

इस तरफ़
is taraf

Turn right.
दायें मुड़ें
dāyen muren.

Turn left.
बायें मुड़ें
bāyen muren.

first (second, third) turn
पहला (दूसरा, तीसरा) मोड़
pahala (dūsara, tīsara) mor

to the right
दाईं ओर
daīn or

to the left
बाईं ओर
baīn or

Go straight ahead.
सीधे जाएं।
sīdhe jaen.

Signs

WELCOME!	स्वागत! svāgat!
ENTRANCE	प्रवेश pravesh
EXIT	निकास nikās
PUSH	पुश, धकेलिए push, dhakelie
PULL	पुल, खींचिए pul, khīnchie
OPEN	खुला khula
CLOSED	बंद band
FOR WOMEN	महिलाओं के लिए mahilaon ke lie
FOR MEN	पुरूषों के लिए purūshon ke lie
GENTLEMEN, GENTS (m)	पुरूष purūsh
WOMEN (f)	महिलाएं mahilaen
DISCOUNTS	छूट chhūt
SALE	सेल sel
FREE	मुफ्त muft
NEW!	नया! naya!
ATTENTION!	ध्यान दें! dhyān den!
NO VACANCIES	कोई कमरा खाली नहीं है koī naukarī nahin hai
RESERVED	रिज़र्वड rizarvad
ADMINISTRATION	प्रबंधन prabandhan
STAFF ONLY	केवल स्टाफ़ keval stāf

BEWARE OF THE DOG! कुत्ते से बचकर रहें!
kutte se bachakar rahen!

NO SMOKING! नो स्मोकिंग!
no smoking!

DO NOT TOUCH! हाथ न लगाएं!
hāth na lagaen!

DANGEROUS खतरनाक
khataranāk

DANGER खतरा
khatara

HIGH VOLTAGE हाई वोल्टेज
haī voltej

NO SWIMMING! स्वीमिंग की अनुमति नहीं है!
svīming kī anumati nahin hai!

OUT OF ORDER ख़राब है
kharāb hai

FLAMMABLE ज्वलनशील
jvalanashīl

FORBIDDEN मनाही
manāhī

NO TRESPASSING! प्रवेश निषेध!
yahān āne kī sakht manāhī hai!

WET PAINT गीला पेंट
gīla pent

CLOSED FOR RENOVATIONS मरम्मत के लिए बंद
marammat ke lie band

WORKS AHEAD आगे कार्य प्रगित पर है
āge kāry pragit par hai

DETOUR डीटूर
dītur

Transportation. General phrases

plane	हवाई जहाज़ havaī jahāz
train	रेलगाड़ी, ट्रेन relagāṛī, tren
bus	बस bas
ferry	फेरी ferī
taxi	टैक्सी taiksī
car	कार kār
schedule	शिड्यूल shidyūl
Where can I see the schedule?	मैं शिड्यूल कहां देख सकता /सकती/ हूं? main shidyūl kahān dekh sakata /sakatī/ hūn?
workdays (weekdays)	कार्यदिवस kāryadivas
weekends	समाहांत saptāhānt
holidays	छुट्टियां chhuttiyān
DEPARTURE	प्रस्थान prasthān
ARRIVAL	आगमन āgaman
DELAYED	देरी derī
CANCELLED	रद्द radd
next (train, etc.)	अगला agala
first	पहला pahala
last	अंतिम antim

When is the next ...?

अगला ... कब है?
agala ... kab hai?

When is the first ...?

पहला ... कब है?
pahala ... kab hai?

When is the last ...?

अंतिम ... कब है?
antim ... kab hai?

---

transfer (change of trains, etc.)

ट्रेन बदलना
tren badalana

to make a transfer

ट्रेन कैसे बदलें
tren kaise badalen

Do I need to make a transfer?

क्या मुझे ट्रेन बदलनी पड़गी?
kya mujhe tren badalanī paragī?

Buying tickets

Where can I buy tickets?	मैं टिकटें कहाँ खरीद सकता /सकती/ हूँ? main tikaten kahān kharīd sakata /sakatī/ hūn?
ticket	टिकट tikat
to buy a ticket	टिकट खरीदना tikat kharīdana
ticket price	टिकट का दाम tikat ka dām
Where to?	कहाँ जाना है? kahān jāna hai?
To what station?	कौन-से स्टेशन के लिए? kaun-se steshan ke lie?
I need ...	मुझे ... चाहिए। mujhe ... chāhie.
one ticket	एक टिकट ek tikat
two tickets	दो टिकट do tikat
three tickets	तीन टिकट tīn tikat
one-way	एक तरफ़ ek taraf
round-trip	राउंड ट्रिप raund trip
first class	फर्स्ट क्लास farst klās
second class	सेकेंड क्लास sekend klās
today	आज āj
tomorrow	कल kal
the day after tomorrow	कल के बाद वाला दिन kal ke bād vāla din
in the morning	सुबह में subah men
in the afternoon	दोपहर में dopahar men
in the evening	शाम में shām men

aisle seat

आयल सीट
āyal sīt

window seat

खिड़की वाली सीट
khirakī vālī sīt

How much?

कितना?
kitana?

Can I pay by credit card?

क्या मैं क्रेडिट कार्ड से पे कर
सकता /सकती/ हूँ?
kya main kredit kārd se pe kar
sakata /sakatī/ hūn?

Bus

bus	बस bas
intercity bus	अंतरराज्यीय बस antararājyīy bas
bus stop	बस-स्टॉप bas-stop
Where's the nearest bus stop?	सबसे करीबी बस-स्टॉप कहाँ है? sabase karībī bas-stop kahān hai?
number (bus ~, etc.)	नंबर nambar
Which bus do I take to get to ...?	... जाने के लिए कौन-सी बस लेनी होगी? ... jāne ke lie kaun-sī bas lenī hogī?
Does this bus go to ...?	क्या यह बस ... जाती है? kya yah bas ... jātī hai?
How frequent are the buses?	बसें कितनी जल्दी-जल्दी आती हैं? basen kitanī jaldī-jaldī ātī hain?
every 15 minutes	हर पंद्रह मिनट har pandrah minat
every half hour	हर आधा घंटा har ādha ghanta
every hour	हर घंटा har ghanta
several times a day	दिन में कई बार din men kaī bār
... times a day	दिन में ... बार din men ... bār
schedule	शिड्यूल shidyūl
Where can I see the schedule?	मैं शिड्यूल कहाँ देख सकता /सकती/ हूँ? main shidyūl kahān dekh sakata /sakatī/ hūn?
When is the next bus?	अगली बस कब है? agalī bas kab hai?
When is the first bus?	पहली बस कब है? pahalī bas kab hai?
When is the last bus?	आखिरी बस कब है? ākhirī bas kab hai?

stop

स्टॉप
stop

next stop

अगला स्टॉप
agala stop

last stop (terminus)

आखिरी स्टॉप
ākhirī stop

Stop here, please.

रोक दें, प्लीज़।
yahān roken, plīz.

Excuse me, this is my stop.

माफ़ कीजिएगा, यह मेरा स्टॉप है।
māf kījiega, yah mera stop hai.

Train

train
रेलगाड़ी, ट्रेन
relagārī, tren

suburban train
लोकल ट्रेन
lokal tren

long-distance train
लंबी दूरी की ट्रेन
lambī dūrī kī tren

train station
ट्रेन स्टेशन
tren steshan

Excuse me, where is the exit to the platform?
माफ़ कीजिएगा, प्लेटफॉर्म से निकलने का रास्ता कहाँ है?
māf kījiega, pletaform se nikalane ka rāsta kahān hai?

Does this train go to ...?
क्या यह ट्रेन ... जाती है?
kya yah tren ... jātī hai?

next train
अगली ट्रेन
agalī tren

When is the next train?
अगली ट्रेन कब है?
agalī tren kab hai?

Where can I see the schedule?
मैं शिड्यूल कहाँ देख सकता /सकती/ हूँ?
main shidyūl kahān dekh sakata /sakatī/ hūn?

From which platform?
कौन-से प्लेटफॉर्म से?
kaun-se pletaform se?

When does the train arrive in ...?
... में ट्रेन कब पहुंचती है?
... men tren kab pahunchatī hai?

Please help me.
कृपया मेरी मदद करें।
kŗpaya merī madad karen.

I'm looking for my seat.
मैं अपनी सीट ढूंढ रहा /रही/ हूँ।
main apanī sīt dhūnrh raha /rahī/ hūn.

We're looking for our seats.
हम अपनी सीट ढूंढ रहे हैं।
ham apanī sīt dhūnrh rahe hain.

My seat is taken.
मेरी सीट पर कोई और बैठा है।
merī sīt par koī aur baitha hai.

Our seats are taken.
हमारी सीटों पर कोई और बैठा है।
hamārī sīton par koī aur baitha hai.

I'm sorry but this is my seat.
माफ़ कीजिएगा, लेकिन यह मेरी सीट है।
māf kījiega, lekin yah merī sīt hai.

Is this seat taken?

क्या इस सीट पर कोई बैठा है?
kya is sīt par koī baitha hai?

May I sit here?

क्या मैं यहाँ बैठ सकता
/सकती/ हूँ?
kya main yahān baith sakata
/sakatī/ hūn?

On the train. Dialogue (No ticket)

Ticket, please.

टिकट, कृपया।
tikat, krpāya.

I don't have a ticket.

मेरे पास टिकट नहीं है।
mere pās tikat nahin hai.

I lost my ticket.

मेरा टिकट खो गया।
mera tikat kho gaya.

I forgot my ticket at home.

मैं अपना टिकट घर पर भूल
गया /गई/।
main apana tikat ghar par bhūl
gaya /gaī/.

You can buy a ticket from me.

आप मुझे एक टिकट दे दें।
āp mujhe ek tikat de den.

You will also have to pay a fine.

आपको फाइन भी भरना होगा।
āpako fain bhī bharana hoga.

Okay.

ठीक है
thīk hai.

Where are you going?

आप कहाँ जा रहे /रही/ हैं?
āp kahān ja rahe /rahī/ hain?

I'm going to ...

मैं ... जा रहा /रही/ हूँ।
main ... ja raha /rahī/ hūn.

How much? I don't understand.

कितना? मैं समझी /समझी/ नहीं।
kitana? main samajhī /samajhī/ nahin.

Write it down, please.

इसे लिख दीजिए, प्लीज़।
ise likh dījie, plīz.

Okay. Can I pay with a credit card?

ठीक है क्या मैं क्रेडिट कार्ड से पे
कर सकता /सकती/ हूँ?
thīk hai. kya main kredit kārd se pe
kar sakata /sakatī/ hūn?

Yes, you can.

हाँ, आप कर सकते हैं।
hān, āp kar sakate hain.

Here's your receipt.

यह रही आपकी रसीद।
yah rahī āpakī rasīd.

Sorry about the fine.

फाइन के बारे में माफ़ कीजिएगा।
fain ke bāre men māf kījiega.

That's okay. It was my fault.

कोई बात नहीं। वह मेरी गलती थी।
koī bāt nahin. vah merī galatī thī.

Enjoy your trip.

अपनी यात्रा का आनंद लें।
apanī yātra ka ānand len.

Taxi

taxi	टैक्सी taiksī
taxi driver	टैक्सी चलाने वाला taiksī chalāne vāla
to catch a taxi	टैक्सी पकड़ना taiksī pakarana
taxi stand	टैक्सी स्टैंड taiksī staind
Where can I get a taxi?	मुझे टैक्सी कहां मिलेगी? mujhe taiksī kahān milegī?

to call a taxi	टैक्सी बुलाना taiksī bulāna
I need a taxi.	मुझे टैक्सी चाहिए mujhe taiksī chāhie.
Right now.	अभी abhī.
What is your address (location)?	आपका पता क्या है? āpaka pata kya hai?
My address is ...	मेरा पता है ... mera pata hai ...
Your destination?	आपको कहाँ जाना है? āpako kahān jāna hai?

Excuse me, ...	माफ़ कीजिएगा, ... māf kījiega, ...
Are you available?	क्या टैक्सी खाली है? kya taiksī khālī hai?
How much is it to get to ...?	... जाने के लिए कितना लगेगा? ... jāne ke lie kitana lagega?
Do you know where it is?	क्या आपको पता है वह कहाँ है? kya āpako pata hai vah kahān hai?

Airport, please.	एयरपोर्ट, प्लीज़ eyaraport, plīz.
Stop here, please.	यहाँ रोकें, प्लीज़ rok den, plīz.
It's not here.	यहाँ नहीं है yahān nahin hai.
This is the wrong address.	यह गलत पता है yah galat pata hai.
Turn left.	बायें मुड़ें bāyen muren.

Turn right.

दायें मुड़ें
dāyen muren.

How much do I owe you?

मुझे आपको कितने पैसे देने हैं?
mujhe āpako kitane paise dene hain?

I'd like a receipt, please.

मैं एक रसीद चाहिए, प्लीज़।
main ek rasīd chāhie, plīz.

Keep the change.

छुट्टे रख लें।
chhutte rakh len.

Would you please wait for me?

क्या आप मेरा इंतज़ार /करेंगे/ करेंगी?
kya āp mera intazār /karenge/ karengī?

five minutes

पाँच मिनट
pānch minat

ten minutes

दस मिनट
das minat

fifteen minutes

पंद्रह मिनट
pandrah minat

twenty minutes

बीस मिनट
bīs minat

half an hour

आधा घंटा
ādhe ghante

Hotel

Hello.	नमस्कार।
	namaskār.
My name is ...	मेरा नाम ... है
	mera nām ... hai
I have a reservation.	मैंने बुकिंग की थी।
	mainne buking kī thī.

I need ...	मुझे ... चाहिए।
	mujhe ... chāhie.
a single room	एक सिंगल कमरा
	ek singal kamara
a double room	एक डबल कमरा
	ek dabal kamara
How much is that?	यह कितने का है?
	yah kitane ka hai?
That's a bit expensive.	यह थोड़ा महंगा है।
	yah thora mahanga hai.

Do you have anything else?	क्या आपके पास कुछ और है?
	kya āpake pās kuchh aur hai?
I'll take it.	मैं यह ले लूँगा /लूँगी/।
	main yah le lūngā /lūngī/.
I'll pay in cash.	मैं नकद दूंगा /दूँगी/।
	main nakad dūngā /dūngī/.

I've got a problem.	मुझे एक परेशानी है।
	mujhe ek pareshānī hai.
My ... is broken.	मेरा ... टूटा हुआ है।
	mera ... tūta hua hai.
My ... is out of order.	मेरा ... ख़राब है।
	mera ... kharāb hai.
TV	टीवी
	tīvī
air conditioner	एयरकंडिशनर
	eyarakandishanar
tap	नल
	nal

shower	शॉवर
	shovar
sink	बेसिन
	besin
safe	तिज़ोरी
	tijorī

door lock	दरवाज़े का ताला
	daravāze ka tāla
electrical outlet	सांकेट
	soket
hairdryer	हेयर ड्रायर
	heyar drāyar

I don't have …	… नहीं है
	… nahin hai
water	पानी
	pānī
light	लाइट
	lait
electricity	बिजली
	bijalī

Can you give me …?	… दे सकते /सकती/ हैं?
	de sakate /sakatī/ hain?
a towel	तौलिया
	tauliya
a blanket	कम्बल
	kambal
slippers	चप्पल
	chappal
a robe	रोब
	rob
shampoo	शैम्पू
	shaimpū
soap	साबुन
	sābun

I'd like to change rooms.	मुझे अपना कमरा बदलना है।
	mujhe apana kamara badalana hai.
I can't find my key.	मुझे चाबी नहीं मिल रही है।
	mujhe chābī nahin mil rahī hai.
Could you open my room, please?	क्या आप मेरा कमरा खोल सकते /सकती/ हैं?
	kya āp mera kamara khol sakate /sakatī/ hain?

Who's there?	कौन है?
	kaun hai?
Come in!	अंदर आ जाओ!
	andar ā jao!
Just a minute!	एक मिनट!
	ek minat!

Not right now, please.	अभी नहीं, प्लीज़।
	abhī nahin, plīz.
Come to my room, please.	कृपया मेरे कमरे में आईये
	kṛpaya mere kamare men āīye.

I'd like to order food service.

मैं फुड सर्विस ऑर्डर करना चाहता
/चाहती/ हूँ।
main fūd sarvis ordar karana chāhata
/chāhatī/ hūn.

My room number is …

मेरा कमरा नंबर है …
mera kamara nambar hai …

I'm leaving …

मैं … जा रहा /रही/ हूँ।
main … ja raha /rahī/ hūn.

We're leaving …

हम … जा रहे हैं।
ham … ja rahe hain.

right now

अभी
abhī

this afternoon

आज दोपहर
āj dopahar

tonight

आज रात
āj rāt

tomorrow

कल
kal

tomorrow morning

कल सुबह
kal subah

tomorrow evening

कल शाम
kal shām

the day after tomorrow

कल के बाद वाला दिन
kal ke bād vāla din

I'd like to pay.

मैं भुगतान करना चाहता
/चाहती/ हूँ।
main bhugatān karana chāhata
/chāhatī/ hūn.

Everything was wonderful.

सब कुछ बहुत अच्छा था।
sab kuchh bahut achchha tha.

Where can I get a taxi?

मुझे टैक्सी कहां मिलेगी?
mujhe taiksī kahān milegī?

Would you call a taxi for me, please?

क्या आप मेरे लिए एक टैक्सी
बुला देंगे /देंगी/?
kya āp mere lie ek taiksī bula
denge /dengī/?

Restaurant

Can I look at the menu, please?

क्या आप अपना मेनू दिखा सकते हैं, प्लीज़?
kya āp apana menū dikha sakate hain, plīz?

Table for one.

एक के लिए टेबल
ek ke lie tebal.

There are two (three, four) of us.

हम दो (तीन, चार) लोग हैं
ham do (tīn, chār) log hain.

Smoking

स्मोकिंग
smoking

No smoking

नो स्मोकिंग
no smoking

Excuse me! (addressing a waiter)

एक्सक्यूज़ मी!
eksakyūz mī!

menu

मेनू
menū

wine list

वाइन सूची
vain sūchī

The menu, please.

मेनू ले आईये प्लीज़।
menū le āiye plīz.

Are you ready to order?

क्या आप ऑर्डर करने के लिए तैयार हैं?
kya āp ordar karane ke lie taiyār hain?

What will you have?

आप क्या लेना चाहेंगी /चाहेंगी/?
āp kya lena chāhengī /chāhengī/?

I'll have ...

मेरे लिए ... ले आईए
mere lie ... le āie.

I'm a vegetarian.

मैं शाकाहारी हूँ।
main shākāhārī hūn.

meat

माँस
māns

fish

मछली
machhalī

vegetables

सब्जियाँ
sabziyān

Do you have vegetarian dishes?

क्या आपके पास शाकाहारी पकवान हैं?
kya āpake pās shākāhārī pakavān hain?

I don't eat pork.

मैं सूअर का गोश्त नहीं खाता /खाती/ हूँ।
main sūar ka gosht nahin khāta /khātī/ hūn.

He /she/ doesn't eat meat.

वह माँस नहीं खाता /खाती/ है।
vah māns nahin khāta /khātī/ hai.

I am allergic to ...

मुझे ... से अलर्जी है।
mujhe ... se alarjī hai.

Would you please bring me ...

क्या आप मेरे लिए ... ले आएंगे प्लीज़
kya āp mere lie ... le āenge plīz

salt | pepper | sugar

नमक | काली मिर्च | चीनी
namak | kālī mirch | chīnī

coffee | tea | dessert

कॉफ़ी | चाय | मीठा
kofī | chāy | mītha

water | sparkling | plain

पानी | बुदबुदाने वाला पानी | सादा
pānī | budabudāne vāla pānī | sāda

a spoon | fork | knife

एक चम्मच | काँटा | चाकू
ek chammach | kānta | chākū

a plate | napkin

एक प्लेट | नैपकिन
ek plet | naipakin

Enjoy your meal!

अपने भोजन का आनंद लें!
apane bhojan ka ānand len!

One more, please.

एक और चाहिए।
ek aur chāhie.

It was very delicious.

वह अत्यंत स्वादिष्ट था।
vah atyant svādisht tha.

check | change | tip

चेक | छुट्टा | टिप
chek | chhutta | tip

Check, please.
(Could I have the check, please?)

चेक प्लीज़।
chek plīz.

Can I pay by credit card?

क्या मैं क्रेडिट कार्ड से पे कर
सकता /सकती/ हूँ
kya main kredit kārd se pe kar sakata
/sakatī/ hūn?

I'm sorry, there's a mistake here.

माफ़ कीजिएगा, यहाँ कुछ गलती है।
māf kījiega, yahān kuchh galatī hai.

Shopping

Can I help you?

क्या मैं आपकी मदद कर सकता /सकती/ हूँ?
kya main āpakī madad kar sakata /sakatī/ hūn?

Do you have ...?

क्या आपके पास ... है?
kya āpake pās ... hai?

I'm looking for ...

मैं ... ढूंढ रहा /रही/ हूँ
main ... dhūnrh raha /rahī/ hūn.

I need ...

मुझे ... चाहिए।
mujhe ... chāhie.

I'm just looking.

मैं बस देख रहा /रही/ हूँ
main bas dekh raha /rahī/ hūn.

We're just looking.

हम बस देख रहे हैं।
ham bas dekh rahe hain.

I'll come back later.

मैं बाद में वापिस आता /आती/ हूँ
main bād men vāpis āta /ātī/ hūn.

We'll come back later.

हम बाद में वापिस आते हैं।
ham bād men vāpis āte hain.

discounts | sale

छूट । सेल
chhūt | sel

Would you please show me ...

क्या आप मुझे ... दिखाएंगे /दिखाएंगी/।
kya āp mujhe ... dikhaenge /dikhaengī/.

Would you please give me ...

क्या आप मुझे ... देंगे /देंगी/।
kya āp mujhe ... denge /dengī/.

Can I try it on?

क्या मैं इसे पहनकर देख सकता /सकती/ हूँ?
kya main ise pahanakar dekh sakata /sakatī/ hūn?

Excuse me, where's the fitting room?

माफ़ कीजिएगा, ट्राय रूम कहाँ है?
māf kījiega, trāy rūm kahān hai?

Which color would you like?

आपको कौन-सा रंग चाहिए?
āpako kaun-sa rang chāhie?

size | length

साइज़ । लंबाई
saiz | lambāī

How does it fit?

यह कैसा फिट होता है?
yah kaisa fit hota hai?

How much is it?

यह कितने का है?
yah kitane ka hai?

That's too expensive.

यह बहुत महंगा है
yah bahut mahanga hai.

I'll take it.

मैं इसे ले लूँगा /लूँगी/।
main ise le lūnga /lūngī/.

Excuse me, where do I pay?

माफ़ कीजिएगा, पे कहाँ करना है?
māf kījiega, pe kahān karana hai?

Will you pay in cash or credit card?

क्या आप नक़द में पे करेंगे या क्रेडिट कार्ड से?
kya āp nakad men pe karenge ya kredit kārd se?

In cash | with credit card

नक़द में | क्रेडिट कार्ड से
nakad men | kredit kārd se

Do you want the receipt?

क्या आपको रसीद चाहिए?
kya āpako rasīd chāhie?

Yes, please.

हाँ, प्लीज़।
hān, plīz.

No, it's OK.

नहीं, ज़रूरत नहीं।
nahin, zarūrat nahin.

Thank you. Have a nice day!

शुक्रिया। आपका दिन शुभ हो।
shukriya. āpaka din shubh ho!

In town

Excuse me, please.	माफ़ कीजिएगा, ... māf kījiega, ...
I'm looking for ...	मैं ... ढूंढ रहा /रही/ हूँ main ... dhūnrh raha /rahī/ hūn.
the subway	मेट्रो metro
my hotel	अपना होटल apana hotal
the movie theater	सिनेमा हॉल sinema hol
a taxi stand	टैक्सी स्टैंड taiksī staind
an ATM	एटीएम etīem
a foreign exchange office	मुद्रा विनिमय केंद्र foran eksachenj ofis
an internet café	साइबर कैफे saibar kaife
... street	... सड़क ... sarak
this place	यह जगह yah jagah
Do you know where ... is?	क्या आपको पता है कि ... कहाँ है? kya āpako pata hai ki ... kahān hai?
Which street is this?	यह कौन-सी सड़क है? yah kaun-sī sarak hai?
Show me where we are right now.	मुझे दिखाईये कि हम इस वक्त कहाँ हैं। mujhe dikhaīye ki ham is vakt kahān hain.
Can I get there on foot?	क्या मैं वहाँ पैदल जा सकता /सकती/ हूँ? kya main vahān paidal ja sakata /sakatī/ hūn?
Do you have a map of the city?	क्या आपके पास शहर का नक्शा है? kya āpake pās shahar ka naksha hai?
How much is a ticket to get in?	अंदर जाने का टिकट कितने का है? andar jāne ka tikat kitane ka hai?
Can I take pictures here?	क्या मैं यहाँ फोटो खींच सकता /सकती/ हूँ? kya main yahān foto khīnch sakata /sakatī/ hūn?

Are you open?

क्या यह जगह खुली है?
kya yah jagah khulī hai?

When do you open?

आप इसे कब खोलते हैं?
āp ise kab kholate hain?

When do you close?

आप इसे कब बंद करते हैं?
āp ise kab band karate hain?

Money

money	पैसा paisa
cash	नकद nakad
paper money	पेपर मनी pepar manī
loose change	सिक्के sikke
check | change | tip	चेक | छुट्टा | टिप chek | chhutta | tip
credit card	क्रेडिट कार्ड kredit kārd
wallet	बटुआ batua
to buy	खरीदना kharīdana
to pay	भुगतान करना bhugatān karana
fine	फाइन fain
free	मुफ्त muft
Where can I buy ...?	मैं ... कहाँ खरीद सकता /सकती/ हूँ? main ... kahā kharīd sakata /sakatī/ hūn?
Is the bank open now?	क्या बैंक इस वक्त खुला होगा? kya baink is vakt khula hoga?
When does it open?	वह कब खुलता है? vah kab khulata hai?
When does it close?	वह कब बंद होता है? vah kab band hota hai?
How much?	कितना? kitana?
How much is this?	यह कितने का है? yah kitane ka hai?
That's too expensive.	यह बहुत महंगा है yah bahut mahanga hai.
Excuse me, where do I pay?	माफ़ कीजिएगा, पे कहाँ करना है? māf kījiega, pe kahān karana hai?

Check, please.

चेक, प्लीज़ा
chek, plīz.

Can I pay by credit card?

क्या मैं क्रेडिट कार्ड से पे कर
सकता /सकती/ हूँ?
kya main kredit kārd se pe kar
sakata /sakatī/ hūn?

Is there an ATM here?

क्या यहाँ पास में एटीएम है?
kya yahān pās men etīem hai?

I'm looking for an ATM.

मैं एटीएम ढूंढ रहा /रही/ हूँ।
main etīem dhūnrh raha /rahī/ hūn.

I'm looking for a foreign exchange office.

मैं मुद्रा विनिमय केंद्र ढूंढ रहा
/रही/ हूँ।
main mudra vinimay kendr dhūnrh raha
/rahī/ hūn.

I'd like to change …

मैं … बदलना चाहूँगा /चाहूँगी/।
main … badalana chāhūnga /chāhūngī/.

What is the exchange rate?

एक्सचेंज रेट क्या है?
eksachenj ret kya hai?

Do you need my passport?

क्या मुझे पासपोर्ट की ज़रूरत है?
kya mujhe pāsaport kī zarūrat hai?

Time

What time is it?	क्या बजा है? kya baja hai?
When?	कब? kab?
At what time?	कितने बजे? kitane baje?
now | later | after ...	अभी | बाद में | ... के बाद abhī | bād men | ... ke bād
one o'clock	एक बजे ek baje
one fifteen	सवा एक बजे sava ek baje
one thirty	डेढ़ बजे derh baje
one forty-five	पौने दो बजे paune do baje

one | two | three	एक | दो | तीन ek | do | tīn
four | five | six	चार | पांच | छह chār | pānch | chhah
seven | eight | nine	सात | आठ | नौ sāt | āth | nau
ten | eleven | twelve	दस | ग्यारह | बारह das | gyārah | bārah

in ...	... में ... men
five minutes	पाँच मिनट pānch minat
ten minutes	दस मिनट das minat
fifteen minutes	पंद्रह मिनट pandrah minat
twenty minutes	बीस मिनट bīs minat
half an hour	आधे घंटे ādha ghanta
an hour	एक घंटे ek ghante
in the morning	सुबह में subah men
early in the morning	सुबह-सेवरे subah-sevare

this morning	इस सुबह
	is subah
tomorrow morning	कल सुबह
	kal subah

in the middle of the day	दोपहर में
	dopahar men
in the afternoon	दोपहर में
	dopahar men
in the evening	शाम में
	shām men
tonight	आज रात
	āj rāt

at night	रात को
	rāt ko
yesterday	कल
	kal
today	आज
	āj
tomorrow	कल
	kal
the day after tomorrow	कल के बाद वाला दिन
	kal ke bād vāla din

What day is it today?	आज कौन-सा दिन है?
	āj kaun-sa din hai?
It's ...	आज ... है
	āj ... hai.
Monday	सोमवार
	somavār
Tuesday	मंगलवार
	mangalavār
Wednesday	बुधवार
	budhavār

Thursday	गुरुवार
	guruvār
Friday	शुक्रवार
	shukravār
Saturday	शनिवार
	shanivār
Sunday	रविवार
	ravivār

Greetings. Introductions

Hello.

नमस्कार
namaskār.

Pleased to meet you.

आपसे मिलकर ख़ुशी हुई
āpase milakar khushī huī.

Me too.

मुझे भी
mujhe bhī.

I'd like you to meet …

मैं आपको … से मिलाना चाहूँगा
/चाहूँगी/।
main āpako … se milāna chāhūnga
/chāhūngī/.

Nice to meet you.

आपसे मिलकर अच्छा लगा।
āpase milakar achchha laga.

How are you?

आप कैसे /कैसी/ हैं?
āp kaise /kaisī/ hain?

My name is …

मेरा नाम … है
mera nām … hai.

His name is …

इसका नाम … है
isaka nām … hai.

Her name is …

इसका नाम … है
isaka nām … hai.

What's your name?

आपका क्या नाम है?
āpaka kya nām hai?

What's his name?

इसका क्या नाम है?
isaka kya nām hai?

What's her name?

इसका क्या नाम है?
isaka kya nām hai?

What's your last name?

आपका आख़िरी नाम क्या है?
āpaka ākhirī nām kya hai?

You can call me …

आप मुझे … बुला सकते /सकती/ हैं
āp mujhe … bula sakate /sakatī/ hain.

Where are you from?

आप कहाँ से हैं?
āp kahān se hain?

I'm from …

मैं … हूँ
main … hūn.

What do you do for a living?

आप क्या काम करते /करती/ हैं?
āp kya kām karate /karatī/ hain?

Who is this?

यह कौन है?
yah kaun hai?

Who is he?

यह कौन है?
yah kaun hai?

Who is she?　　यह कौन है?
　　　　　　　yah kaun hai?

Who are they?　ये कौन हैं?
　　　　　　　ye kaun hain?

This is …　　　यह … है।
　　　　　　　yah … hai.

my friend (masc.)　मेरा दोस्त
　　　　　　　mera dost

my friend (fem.)　मेरी सहेली
　　　　　　　merī sahelī

my husband　　मेरे पति
　　　　　　　mere pati

my wife　　　मेरी पत्नी
　　　　　　　merī patnī

my father　　　मेरे पिता
　　　　　　　mere pita

my mother　　मेरी माँ
　　　　　　　merī mān

my brother　　मेरे भाई
　　　　　　　mere bhaī

my sister　　　मेरी बहन
　　　　　　　merī bahan

my son　　　　मेरा बेटा
　　　　　　　mera beta

my daughter　　मेरी बेटी
　　　　　　　merī betī

This is our son.　यह मेरा बेटा है।
　　　　　　　yah mera beta hai.

This is our daughter.　यह मेरी बेटी है।
　　　　　　　yah merī betī hai.

These are my children.　ये मेरे बच्चे हैं।
　　　　　　　ye mere bachche hain.

These are our children.　ये हमारे बच्चे हैं।
　　　　　　　ye hamāre bachche hain.

Farewells

Good bye!
अलविदा!
alavida!

Bye! (inform.)
बाय!
bāy!

See you tomorrow.
कल मिलते हैं
kal milate hain.

See you soon.
जल्दी मिलते हैं
jaldī milate hain.

See you at seven.
सात बजे मिलते हैं
sāt baje milate hain.

Have fun!
मज़े करो!
maze karo!

Talk to you later.
बाद में बात करते हैं
bād men bāt karate hain.

Have a nice weekend.
तुम्हारा सप्ताहांत शुभ रहे
tumhāra saptāhānt shubh rahe.

Good night.
शुभ रात्रि
shubh rātri.

It's time for me to go.
मेरे जाने का वक्त हो गया है
mere jāne ka vakt ho gaya hai.

I have to go.
मुझे जाना होगा
mujhe jāna hai.

I will be right back.
मैं अभी वापिस आता /आती/ हूँ
main abhī vāpis āta /ātī/ hūn.

It's late.
देर हो गई है
der ho gaī hai.

I have to get up early.
मुझे जल्दी उठना है
mujhe jaldī uthana hai.

I'm leaving tomorrow.
मैं कल जाने वाला /वाली/ हूँ
main kal jāne vāla /vālī/ hūn.

We're leaving tomorrow.
हम कल जाने वाले हैं
ham kal jāne vāle hain.

Have a nice trip!
आपकी यात्रा शानदार हो!
āpakī yātra shānadār ho!

It was nice meeting you.
आपसे मिलकर अच्छा लगा
āpase milakar achchha laga.

It was nice talking to you.
आपसे बातें करके अच्छा लगा
āpase bāten karake achchha laga.

Thanks for everything.
हर चीज़ के लिए शुक्रिया
har chīz ke lie shukriya.

I had a very good time.

मैंने बहुत अच्छा वक्त बिताया।
mainne bahut achchha vakt bitāya.

We had a very good time.

हमने बहुत अच्छा वक्त बिताया।
hamane bahut achchha vakt bitāya.

It was really great.

बहुत मज़ा आया।
bahut maza āya.

I'm going to miss you.

मुझे तुम्हारी याद आएगी।
mujhe tumhārī yād āegī.

We're going to miss you.

हमें आपकी याद आएगी।
hamen āpakī yād āegī.

Good luck!

गुड लक!
gud lak!

Say hi to ...

... को नमस्ते बोलना।
... ko namaste bolana.

Foreign language

I don't understand.	मुझे समझ नहीं आया। mujhe samajh nahin āya.
Write it down, please.	इसे लिख दीजिए, प्लीज़। ise likh dījie, plīz.
Do you speak ...?	क्या आप ... बोलते /बोलती/ हैं? kya āp ... bolate /bolatī/ hain?
I speak a little bit of ...	मैं थोड़ा-बहुत ... बोल सकता /सकती/ हूँ। main thora-bahut ... bol sakata /sakatī/ hūn.
English	अंग्रेज़ी angrezī
Turkish	तुर्की turkī
Arabic	अरबी arabī
French	फ़्रांसिसी frānsisī
German	जर्मन jarman
Italian	इतालवी itālavī
Spanish	स्पेनी spenī
Portuguese	पुर्तगाली purtagālī
Chinese	चीनी chīnī
Japanese	जापानी jāpānī
Can you repeat that, please.	क्या आप इसे दोहरा सकते हैं kya āp ise dohara sakate hain.
I understand.	मैं समझ गया /गई/। main samajh gaya /gaī/.
I don't understand.	मुझे समझ नहीं आया। mujhe samajh nahin āya.
Please speak more slowly.	कृपया थोड़ा और धीरे बोलिये। krpaya thora aur dhīre boliye.

Is that correct? (Am I saying it right?)   **क्या यह सही है?**
kya yah sahī hai?

What is this? (What does this mean?)   **यह क्या है?**
yah kya hai?

Apologies

Excuse me, please.

मुझे माफ़ करना।
mujhe māf karana.

I'm sorry.

मुझे माफ़ कर दो।
mujhe māf karana.

I'm really sorry.

मैं बहुत शर्मिन्दा हूँ।
main bahut sharminda hūn.

Sorry, it's my fault.

माफ़ करना, यह मेरी गलती है।
māf karana, yah merī galatī hai.

My mistake.

मेरी गलती।
merī galatī.

May I ...?

क्या मैं ... सकता /सकती/ हूँ?
kya main ... sakata /sakatī/ hūn?

Do you mind if I ...?

क्या मैं ... सकता /सकती/ हूँ?
kya main ... sakata /sakatī/ hūn?

It's OK.

कोई बात नहीं।
koī bāt nahin.

It's all right.

सब कुछ ठीक है।
sab kuchh thīk hai.

Don't worry about it.

फ़िक्र मत करो।
fikr mat karo.

Agreement

Yes.
हाँ।
hān.

Yes, sure.
हाँ, बिल्कुल।
hān, bilkul.

OK (Good!)
ओके! बढ़िया!
oke! barhiya!

Very well.
ठीक है।
thīk hai.

Certainly!
बिल्कुल!
bilkul!

I agree.
मैं सहमत हूँ।
main sahamat hūn.

That's correct.
यह सही है।
yah sahī hai.

That's right.
यह ठीक है।
yah thīk hai.

You're right.
आप सही हैं।
āp sahī hain.

I don't mind.
मुझे बुरा नहीं लगेगा।
mujhe bura nahin lagega.

Absolutely right.
बिल्कुल सही।
bilkul sahī.

It's possible.
हो सकता है।
ho sakata hai.

That's a good idea.
यह अच्छा विचार है।
yah achchha vichār hai.

I can't say no.
मैं नहीं नहीं बोल सकता
/सकती/ हूँ।
main nahin nahin bol sakata
/sakatī/ hūn.

I'd be happy to.
मुझे खुश होगी।
mujhe khush hogī.

With pleasure.
खुशी से।
khushī se.

Refusal. Expressing doubt

No.	नहीं। nahin.
Certainly not.	बिल्कुल नहीं। bilkul nahin.
I don't agree.	मैं सहमत नहीं हूँ। main sahamat nahin hūn.
I don't think so.	मुझे नहीं लगता है। mujhe nahin lagata hai.
It's not true.	यह सही नहीं है। yah sahī nahin hai.

You are wrong.	आप गलत हैं। āp galat hain.
I think you are wrong.	मेरे ख्याल में आप गलत हैं। mere khyāl men āp galat hain.
I'm not sure.	मुझे पक्का नहीं पता है। mujhe pakka nahin pata hai.
It's impossible.	यह मुमकिन नहीं है। yah mumakin nahin hai.
Nothing of the kind (sort)!	ऐसा कुछ नहीं हुआ! aisa kuchh nahin hua!

The exact opposite.	इससे बिल्कुल उलटा। isase bilkul ulata.
I'm against it.	मैं इसके खिलाफ़ हूँ। main isake khilāf hūn.
I don't care.	मुझे कोई फर्क नहीं पड़ता। mujhe koī fark nahin parata.
I have no idea.	मुझे कुछ नहीं पता। mujhe kuchh nahin pata.
I doubt it.	मुझे इस बात पर शक है। mujhe is bāt par shak hai.

Sorry, I can't.	माफ़ करना, मैं नहीं कर सकता /सकती/ हूँ। māf karana, main nahin kar sakata /sakatī/ hūn.
Sorry, I don't want to.	माफ़ करना, मैं नहीं करना चाहता /चाहती/ हूँ। māf karana, main nahin karana chāhata /chāhatī/ hūn.
Thank you, but I don't need this.	शुक्रिया, मगर मुझे इसकी ज़रूरत नहीं है। shukriya, magar mujhe isakī zarūrat nahin hai.

It's getting late.

देर हो रही है।
der ho rahī hai.

I have to get up early.

मुझे जल्दी उठना है
mujhe jaldī uthana hai.

I don't feel well.

मेरी तबियत ठीक नहीं है।
merī tabiyat thīk nahin hai.

Expressing gratitude

Thank you.	शुक्रिया। shukriya.
Thank you very much.	बहुत बहुत शुक्रिया। bahut bahut shukriya.
I really appreciate it.	मैं बहुत आभारी हूँ। main bahut ābhārī hūn.
I'm really grateful to you.	मैं बहुत बहुत आभारी हूँ। main bahut bahut ābhārī hūn.
We are really grateful to you.	हम बहुत आभारी हैं। ham bahut ābhārī hain.
Thank you for your time.	आपके वक्त के लिए शुक्रिया। āpake vakt ke lie shukriya.
Thanks for everything.	हर चीज़ के लिए शुक्रिया। har chīz ke lie shukriya.
Thank you for ...	... के लिए शुक्रिया। ... ke lie shukriya.
your help	आपकी मदद āpakī madad
a nice time	अच्छे वक्त achchhe vakt
a wonderful meal	बढ़िया खाने barhiya khāne
a pleasant evening	खुशनुमा शाम khushanuma shām
a wonderful day	बढ़िया दिन barhiya din
an amazing journey	अद्भुत सफर adbhut safar
Don't mention it.	शुक्रिया की कोई ज़रूरत नहीं। shukriya kī koī zarūrat nahin.
You are welcome.	आपका स्वागत है। āpaka svāgat hai.
Any time.	कभी भी। kabhī bhī.
My pleasure.	यह मेरे लिए खुशी की बात है। yah mere lie khushī kī bāt hai.
Forget it.	भूल जाओ। bhūl jao.
Don't worry about it.	फिक्र मत करो। fikr mat karo.

Congratulations. Best wishes

Congratulations!
मुबारक हो!
mubārak ho!

Happy birthday!
जन्मदिन की बधाई!
janmadin kī badhaī!

Merry Christmas!
बड़ा दिन मुबारक हो!
bara din mubārak ho!

Happy New Year!
नए साल की बधाई!
nae sāl kī badhaī!

Happy Easter!
ईस्टर की शुभकामनाएं!
īstar kī shubhakāmanaen!

Happy Hanukkah!
हनुका की बधाईयाँ!
hanuka kī badhaīyān!

I'd like to propose a toast.
मैं एक टोस्ट करना चाहूँगा /चाहूँगी/।
main ek tost karana chāhūnga /chāhūngī/.

Cheers!
चियर्स!
chiyars!

Let's drink to ...!
... के लिए पीया जाए!
... ke lie pīya jae!

To our success!
हमारी कामियाबी!
hamārī kāmiyābī!

To your success!
आपकी कामियाबी!
āpakī kāmiyābī!

Good luck!
गुड लक!
gud lak!

Have a nice day!
आपका दिन शुभ हो!
āpaka din shubh ho!

Have a good holiday!
आपकी छुट्टी अच्छी रहे!
āpakī chhuttī achchhī rahe!

Have a safe journey!
आपका सफर सुरक्षित रहे!
āpaka safar surakshit rahe!

I hope you get better soon!
मैं उम्मीद करता /करती/ हूँ कि आप जल्द ही ठीक हो जाएंगे!
main ummīd karata /karatī/ hūn ki āp jald hī thīk ho jaenge!

Socializing

Why are you sad?

आप उदास क्यों हैं?
āp udās kyon hain?

Smile! Cheer up!

मुस्कुराओ! खुश रहो!
muskurao! khush raho!

Are you free tonight?

क्या आप आज रात फ्री हैं?
kya āp āj rāt frī hain?

May I offer you a drink?

क्या मैं आपके लिए एक ड्रिंक खरीद
सकता /सकती/ हूँ?
kya main āpake lie ek drink kharīd
sakata /sakatī/ hūn?

Would you like to dance?

क्या आप डांस करना चाहेंगी
/चाहेंगी/?
kya āp dāns karana chāhengī
/chāhengī/?

Let's go to the movies.

चलिए फ़िल्म देखने चलते हैं.
chalie film dekhane chalate hain.

May I invite you to …?

क्या मैं आपको … इन्वाइट
कर सकता /सकती/ हूँ?
kya main āpako … invait
kar sakata /sakatī/ hūn?

a restaurant

रेस्तरां
restarān

the movies

फ़िल्म के लिए
film ke lie

the theater

थियेटर के लिए
thiyetar ke lie

go for a walk

वॉक के लिए
vok ke lie

At what time?

कितने बजे?
kitane baje?

tonight

आज रात
āj rāt

at six

छह बजे
chhah baje

at seven

सात बजे
sāt baje

at eight

आठ बजे
āth baje

at nine

नौ बजे
nau baje

Do you like it here?	क्या आपको यहाँ अच्छा लगता है? kya āpako yahān achchha lagata hai?
Are you here with someone?	क्या आप यहाँ किसी के साथ आए /आई/ हैं? kya āp yahān kisī ke sāth āe /āī/ hain?
I'm with my friend.	मैं अपने दोस्त के साथ हूँ। main apane dost ke sāth hūn.
I'm with my friends.	मैं अपने दोस्तों के साथ हूँ। main apane doston ke sāth hūn.
No, I'm alone.	नहीं, मैं अकेला /अकेली/ हूँ। nahin, main akela /akelī/ hūn.
Do you have a boyfriend?	क्या आपका कोई बॉयफ्रेंड है? kya āpaka koī boyafrend hai?
I have a boyfriend.	मेरा बॉयफ्रेंड है। mera boyafrend hai.
Do you have a girlfriend?	क्या आपकी कोई गर्लफ्रेंड है? kya āpakī koī garlafrend hai?
I have a girlfriend.	मेरी एक गर्लफ्रेंड है। merī ek garlafrend hai.
Can I see you again?	क्या आपसे फिर मिल सकता /सकती/ हूँ? kya āpase fir mil sakata /sakatī/ hūn?
Can I call you?	क्या मैं आपको कॉल कर सकता /सकती/ हूँ? kya main āpako kol kar sakata /sakatī/ hūn?
Call me. (Give me a call.)	मुझे कॉल करना। mujhe kol karana.
What's your number?	आपका नंबर क्या है? āpaka nambar kya hai?
I miss you.	मुझे तुम्हारी याद आ रही है। mujhe tumhārī yād ā rahī hai.
You have a beautiful name.	आपका नाम बहुत खूबसूरत है। āpaka nām bahut khūbasūrat hai.
I love you.	मैं तुमसे प्यार करता /करती/ हूँ। main tumase pyār karata /karatī/ hūn.
Will you marry me?	क्या तुम मुझसे शादी करोगे /करोगी/? kya tum mujhase shādī karoge /karogī/?
You're kidding!	तुम मज़ाक कर रहे /रही/ हो! tum mazāk kar rahe /rahī/ ho!
I'm just kidding.	मैं बस मज़ाक कर रहा रही हूँ। main bas mazāk kar raha rahī hūn.
Are you serious?	क्या आप सीरियस हैं? kya āp sīriyas hain?
I'm serious.	मैं सीरियस हूँ। main sīriyas hūn.

Really?! | सच में?!
| sach men?!

It's unbelievable! | मुझे यकिन नहीं होता!
| mujhe yakin nahin hota!

I don't believe you. | मुझे तुम पर यकिन नहीं है
| mujhe tum par yakin nahin hai.

I can't. | मैं नहीं आ सकता /सकती/।
| main nahin ā sakata /sakatī/.

I don't know. | मुझे नहीं मालूम।
| mujhe nahin mālūm.

I don't understand you. | मुझे आपकी बात समझ नहीं आई
| mujhe āpakī bāt samajh nahin āī.

Please go away. | यहाँ से चले जाईये
| yahān se chale jaīye.

Leave me alone! | मुझे अकेला छोड़ दो!
| mujhe akela chhor do!

I can't stand him. | मैं उसे बदार्शत नहीं कर सकता /सकती/ हूँ
| main use bardāsht nahin kar sakata /sakatī/ hūn.

You are disgusting! | तुमसे चिन्न आती है!
| tumase ghinn ātī hai!

I'll call the police! | मैं पुलिस बुला लूँगा /लूँगी/!
| main pulis bula lūnga /lūngī/!

Sharing impressions. Emotions

I like it.	मुझे यह पसंद है। mujhe yah pasand hai.
Very nice.	बहुत अच्छा। bahut achchha.
That's great!	बहुत बढ़िया! bahut barhiya!
It's not bad.	बुरा नहीं है। bura nahin hai.
I don't like it.	मुझे यह पसंद नहीं है। mujhe yah pasand nahin hai.
It's not good.	यह अच्छा नहीं है। yah achchha nahin hai.
It's bad.	यह बुरा है। yah bura hai.
It's very bad.	यह बहुत बुरा है। yah bahut bura hai.
It's disgusting.	यह घिनौना है। yah ghinauna hai.
I'm happy.	मैं खुश हूँ। main khush hūn.
I'm content.	मैं संतुष्ट हूँ। main santusht hūn.
I'm in love.	मुझे प्यार हो गया है। mujhe pyār ho gaya hai.
I'm calm.	मैं शांत हूँ। main shānt hūn.
I'm bored.	मुझे बोरियत हो रही है। mujhe boriyat ho rahī hai.
I'm tired.	मैं थक गया /गई/ हूँ। main thak gaya /gaī/ hūn.
I'm sad.	मैं दुखी हूँ। main dukhī hūn.
I'm frightened.	मुझे डर लग रहा है। mujhe dar lag raha hain.
I'm angry.	मुझे गुस्सा आ रहा है। mujhe gussa ā raha hai.
I'm worried.	मैं परेशान हूँ। main pareshān hūn.
I'm nervous.	मुझे घवराहट हो रही है। mujhe ghavarāhat ho rahī hai.

I'm jealous. (envious)

मुझे जलन हो रही है
mujhe jalan ho rahī hai.

I'm surprised.

मुझे हैरानी हो रही है।
mujhe hairānī ho rahī hai.

I'm perplexed.

मुझे समझ नहीं आ रहा है।
mujhe samajh nahin ā raha hai.

Problems. Accidents

I've got a problem.
मुझे एक परेशानी है।
mujhe ek pareshānī hai.

We've got a problem.
हमें परेशानी है।
hamen pareshānī hai.

I'm lost.
मैं खो गया /गई/ हूँ।
main kho gaya /gaī/ hūn.

I missed the last bus (train).
मुझसे आखिरी बस छूट गई।
mujhase ākhirī bas chhūt gaī.

I don't have any money left.
मेरे पास पैसे नहीं बचे।
mere pās paise nahin bache.

I've lost my ...
मेरा ... खो गया है।
mera ... kho gaya hai.

Someone stole my ...
किसी ने मेरा ... चुरा लिया।
kisī ne mera ... chura liya.

passport
पासपोर्ट
pāsaport

wallet
बटुआ
batua

papers
कागज़ात
kāgazāt

ticket
टिकट
tikat

money
पैसा
paisa

handbag
पर्स
pars

camera
कैमरा
kaimara

laptop
लैपटॉप
laipatop

tablet computer
टैबलेट
taibalet

mobile phone
मोबाइल फ़ोन
mobail fon

Help me!
मेरी मदद करो!
merī madad karo!

What's happened?
क्या हुआ?
kya hua?

fire
आग
āg

shooting
गोलियाँ चल रही हैं
goliyān chal rahī hain

murder
कत्ल हो गया है
katl ho gaya hai

explosion
विस्फोट हो गया है
visfot ho gaya hai

fight
लड़ाई हो गई है
laraī ho gaī hai

Call the police!
पुलिस को बुलाओ!
pulis ko bulāo!

Please hurry up!
कृपया जल्दी करें!
kṛpaya jaldī karen!

I'm looking for the police station.
मैं पुलिस थाना ढूंढ रहा /रही/ हूँ।
main pulis thāna dhūnrh raha /rahī/ hūn.

I need to make a call.
मुझे फ़ोन करना है
mujhe fon karana hai.

May I use your phone?
क्या मैं आपका फ़ोन इस्तेमाल
कर सकता /सकती/ हूँ?
kya main āpaka fon istemāl
kar sakata /sakatī/ hūn?

mugged
मेरा सामान चुरा लिया गया है
mera sāmān chura liya gaya hai

robbed
मुझे लूट लिया गया है
mujhe lūt liya gaya hai

raped
मेरा बालात्कार किया गया है
mera bālātkār kiya gaya hai

attacked (beaten up)
मुझे पीटा गया है
mujhe pīta gaya hai

Are you all right?
क्या आप ठीक हैं?
kya āp thīk hain?

Did you see who it was?
क्या आपने देखा कौन था?
kya āpane dekha kaun tha?

Would you be able to recognize
the person?
क्या आप उसे पहचान सकेंगे
/सकेंगी/?
kya āp use pahachān sakenge
/sakengī/?

Are you sure?
क्या आपको यकीन है?
kya āpako yakīn hai?

Please calm down.
कृपया शांत हो जाएं
kṛpaya shānt ho jaen.

Take it easy!
आराम से!
ārām se!

Don't worry!
चिंता मत करो!
chinta mat karo!

Everything will be fine.
सब ठीक हो जायेगा।
sab thīk ho jāyega.

Everything's all right.
सब कुछ ठीक है।
sab kuchh thīk hai.

Come here, please.
कृपया यहाँ आइये।
kṛpaya yahān āiye.

I have some questions for you.	मेरे पास तुम्हारे लिए कुछ प्रश्न है।
	mere pās tumhāre lie kuchh prashn hai.
Wait a moment, please.	कृपया एक क्षण रुकें।
	kṛpaya ek kshan ruken.
Do you have any I.D.?	क्या आपके पास आईडी है?
	kya āpake pās āīdī hai?
Thanks. You can leave now.	धन्यवाद। आप अब जा सकते /सकती/ हैं।
	dhanyavād. āp ab ja sakate /sakatī/ hain.
Hands behind your head!	अपने हाथ सिर के पीछे रखें!
	apane hāth sir ke pīchhe rakhen!
You're under arrest!	आप हिरासत में हैं!
	āp hirāsat men hain!

Health problems

Please help me.

कृपया मेरी मदद करें।
krpaya merī madad karen.

I don't feel well.

मेरी तबियत ठीक नहीं है
merī tabiyat thīk nahin hai.

My husband doesn't feel well.

मेरे पति को ठीक महसूस नहीं
हो रहा है।
mere pati ko thīk mahasūs nahin
ho raha hai.

My son ...

मेरे बेटे ...
mere bete ...

My father ...

मेरे पिता ...
mere pita ...

My wife doesn't feel well.

मेरी पत्नी को ठीक महसूस नहीं
हो रहा है।
merī patnī ko thīk mahasūs nahin
ho raha hai.

My daughter ...

मेरी बेटी ...
merī betī ...

My mother ...

मेरी माँ ...
merī mān ...

headache

मुझे सिरदर्द है।
mujhe siradard hai.

sore throat

मेरा गला ख़राब है।
mera gala kharāb hai.

stomach ache

मेरे पेट में दर्द है।
mere pet men dard hai.

toothache

मेरे दाँत में दर्द है।
mere dānt men dard hai.

I feel dizzy.

मुझे चक्कर आ रहा है।
mujhe chakkar ā raha hai.

He has a fever.

इसे बुखार है।
ise bukhār hai.

She has a fever.

इसे बुखार है।
ise bukhār hai.

I can't breathe.

मैं साँस नहीं ले पा रहा /रही/ हूँ।
main sāns nahin le pa raha /rahī/ hūn.

I'm short of breath.

मेरी साँस फूल रही है।
merī sāns fūl rahī hai.

I am asthmatic.

मुझे दमा है।
mujhe dama hai.

I am diabetic.

मैं मधुमेह का /की/ रोगी हूँ।
main madhumeh ka /kī/ rogī hūn.

I can't sleep.

मैं सो नहीं पा रहा /रही/ हूँ।
main so nahin pa raha /rahī/ hūn.

food poisoning

फ़ूड पॉएज़निंग
fūd poezaning

It hurts here.

यहाँ दुखता हैं।
yahān dukhata hain.

Help me!

मेरी मदद करो!
merī madad karo!

I am here!

मैं यहाँ हूँ!
main yahān hūn!

We are here!

हम यहाँ हैं।
ham yahān hain!

Get me out of here!

मुझे यहां से बाहर निकालो!
mujhe yahān se bāhar nikālo!

I need a doctor.

मुझे एक डॉक्टर की ज़रुरत है।
mujhe ek doktar kī zarurat hai.

I can't move.

मैं हिल नहीं सकता /सकती/ हूँ।
main hil nahin sakata /sakatī/ hūn.

I can't move my legs.

मैं अपने पैरों को नहीं हिला
पा रहा /रही/ हूँ।
main apane pairon ko nahin hila
pa raha /rahī/ hūn.

I have a wound.

मुझे चोट लगी है।
mujhe chot lagī hai.

Is it serious?

क्या यह गंभीर है?
kya yah gambhīr hai?

My documents are in my pocket.

मेरे दस्तावेज़ मेरी जेब में हैं।
mere dastāvez merī jeb men hain.

Calm down!

शांत हो जाओ!
shānt ho jao!

May I use your phone?

क्या मैं आपका फ़ोन इस्तेमाल
कर सकता /सकती/ हूँ?
kya main āpaka fon istemāl
kar sakata /sakatī/ hūn?

Call an ambulance!

एम्बुलेन्स बुलाओ!
embulens bulao!

It's urgent!

बहुत ज़रूरी है।
bahut zarūrī hai!

It's an emergency!

यह एक आपातकाल है!
yah ek āpātakāl hai!

Please hurry up!

कृपया जल्दी करें!
krpaya jaldī karen!

Would you please call a doctor?

क्या आप डॉक्टर को बुला देंगे /देंगी/?
kya āp doktar ko bula denge /dengī/?

Where is the hospital?

अस्पताल कहाँ है?
aspatāl kahān hai?

How are you feeling?

आप कैसा महसूस कर रहे /रही/ हैं?
āp kaisa mahasūs kar rahe /rahī/ hain?

Are you all right?

क्या आप ठीक हैं?
kya āp thīk hain?

What's happened?

क्या हुआ?
kya hua?

I feel better now.

मैं अब ठीक हूँ।
main ab thīk hūn.

It's OK.

सब ठीक है।
sab thīk hai.

It's all right.

सब कुछ ठीक है।
sab kuchh thīk hai.

At the pharmacy

pharmacy (drugstore)

दवा की दुकान
dava kī dukān

24-hour pharmacy

चौबीस घंटे खुलने वाली
दवा की दुकान
chaubīs ghante khulane vālī
dava kī dukān

Where is the closest pharmacy?

सबसे करीबी दवा की दुकान कहाँ है?
sabase karībī dava kī dukān kahān hai?

Is it open now?

क्या वह अभी खुली है?
kya vah abhī khulī hai?

At what time does it open?

वह कितने बजे खुलती है?
vah kitane baje khulatī hai?

At what time does it close?

वह कितने बजे बंद होती है?
vah kitane baje band hotī hai?

Is it far?

क्या वह दूर है?
kya vah dūr hai?

Can I get there on foot?

क्या मैं वहाँ पैदल जा सकता
/सकती/ हूँ?
kya main vahān paidal ja sakata
/sakatī/ hūn?

Can you show me on the map?

क्या आप मुझे नक्शे पर दिखा
सकते /सकती/ हैं?
kya āp mujhe nakshe par dikha
sakate /sakatī/ hain?

Please give me something for ...

मुझे ... के लिए कुछ दे दें।
mujhe ... ke lie kuchh de den.

a headache

सिरदर्द
siradard

a cough

खाँसी
khānsī

a cold

जुकाम
zukām

the flu

जुकाम-बुखार
zukām-bukhār

a fever

बुखार
bukhār

a stomach ache

पेट दर्द
pet dard

nausea

मतली
matalī

diarrhea	दस्त dast
constipation	कब्ज़ kabz

pain in the back	पीठ दर्द pīth dard
chest pain	सीने में दर्द sīne men dard
side stitch	पेट की माँसपेशी में दर्द pet kī mānsapeshī men dard
abdominal pain	पेट दर्द pet dard

pill	दवा dava
ointment, cream	मरहम, क्रीम maraham, krīm
syrup	सिरप sirap
spray	स्प्रे spre
drops	ड्रॉप drop

You need to go to the hospital.	आपको अस्पताल जाना चाहिए। āpako aspatāl jāna chāhie.
health insurance	स्वास्थ्य बीमा svāsthy bīma
prescription	नुस्खा nuskha
insect repellant	कीटरोधक kītarodhak
Band Aid	बैंड एड baind ed

The bare minimum

Excuse me, ...	माफ़ कीजिएगा, ... māf kījiega, ...
Hello.	नमस्कार। namaskār.
Thank you.	शुक्रिया। shukriya.
Good bye.	अलविदा। alavida.
Yes.	हाँ। hān.
No.	नहीं। nahin.
I don't know.	मुझे नहीं मालूम। mujhe nahin mālūm.
Where? | Where to? | When?	कहाँ? | कहाँ जाना है? | कब? kahān? | kahān jāna hai? | kab?

I need ...	मुझे ... चाहिए। mujhe ... chāhie.
I want ...	मैं ... चाहता /चाहती/ हूँ। main ... chāhata /chāhatī/ hūn.
Do you have ...?	क्या आपके पास ... है? kya āpake pās ... hai?
Is there a ... here?	क्या यहाँ ... है? kya yahān ... hai?
May I ...?	क्या मैं ... सकता /सकती/ हूँ? kya main ... sakata /sakatī/ hūn?
..., please (polite request)	..., कृपया। ..., krpaya.

I'm looking for ...	मैं ... ढूंढ रहा /रही/ हूँ। main ... dhūnrh raha /rahī/ hūn.
restroom	शौचालय shauchālay
ATM	एटीएम etīem
pharmacy (drugstore)	दवा की दुकान dava kī dūkān
hospital	अस्पताल aspatāl
police station	पुलिस थाना pulis thāna
subway	मेट्रो metro

taxi	टैक्सी taiksī
train station	ट्रेन स्टेशन tren steshan

My name is ...	मेरा नाम ... है। mera nām ... hai
What's your name?	आपका क्या नाम है? āpaka kya nām hai?
Could you please help me?	क्या आप मेरी मदद कर सकते /सकती/ हैं? kya āp merī madad kar sakate /sakatī/ hain?
I've got a problem.	मुझे एक परेशानी है। mujhe ek pareshānī hai.
I don't feel well.	मेरी तबियत ठीक नहीं है। merī tabiyat thīk nahin hai.
Call an ambulance!	एम्बुलेन्स बुलाओ! embulens bulao!
May I make a call?	क्या मैं एक फ़ोन कर सकता /सकती/ हैं? kya main ek fon kar sakata /sakatī/ hūn?

I'm sorry.	मुझे माफ़ करना। mujhe māf kar do.
You're welcome.	आपका स्वागत है। āpaka svāgat hai.

I, me	मैं main
you (inform.)	तू tū
he	वह vah
she	वह vah
they (masc.)	वे ve
they (fem.)	वे ve
we	हम ham
you (pl)	तुम tum
you (sg, form.)	आप āp

ENTRANCE	प्रवेश pravesh
EXIT	निकास nikās

OUT OF ORDER   ख़राब है
kharāb hai

CLOSED   बंद
band

OPEN   खुला
khula

FOR WOMEN   महिलाओं के लिए
mahilaon ke lie

FOR MEN   पुरूषों के लिए
purūshon ke lie

MINI DICTIONARY

This section contains 250
useful words required for
everyday communication.
You will find the names of
months and days of the week
here. The dictionary also
contains topics such as colors,
measurements, family, and
more

T&P Books Publishing

DICTIONARY CONTENTS

T&P Books Publishing

time	वक्त (m)	vakt
hour	घंटा (m)	ghanta
half an hour	आधा घंटा	ādha ghanta
minute	मिनट (m)	minat
second	सेकन्ड (m)	sekand
today (adv)	आज	āj
tomorrow (adv)	कल	kal
yesterday (adv)	कल	kal
Monday	सोमवार (m)	somavār
Tuesday	मंगलवार (m)	mangalavār
Wednesday	बुधवार (m)	budhavār
Thursday	गुरूवार (m)	gurūvār
Friday	शुक्रवार (m)	shukravār
Saturday	शनिवार (m)	shanivār
Sunday	रविवार (m)	ravivār
day	दिन (m)	din
working day	कार्यदिवस (m)	kāryadivas
public holiday	सार्वजनिक छुट्टी (f)	sārvajanik chhuttī
weekend	सप्ताहांत (m)	saptāhānt
week	हफ़ता (f)	hafata
last week (adv)	पिछले हफ़ते	pichhale hafate
next week (adv)	अगले हफ़ते	agale hafate
in the morning	सुबह में	subah men
in the afternoon	दोपहर में	dopahar men
in the evening	शाम में	shām men
tonight (this evening)	आज शाम	āj shām
at night	रात में	rāt men
midnight	आधी रात (f)	ādhī rāt
January	जनवरी (m)	janavarī
February	फ़रवरी (m)	faravarī
March	मार्च (m)	mārch
April	अप्रैल (m)	aprail
May	माई (m)	maī
June	जून (m)	jūn
July	जुलाई (m)	julaī
August	अगस्त (m)	agast

September	सितम्बर (m)	sitambar
October	अक्तूबर (m)	aktūbar
November	नवम्बर (m)	navambar
December	दिसम्बर (m)	disambar

in spring	वसन्त में	vasant men
in summer	गरमियों में	garamiyon men
in fall	शरद में	sharad men
in winter	सर्दियों में	sardiyon men

month	महीना (m)	mahīna
season (summer, etc.)	मौसम (m)	mausam
year	वर्ष (m)	varsh

2. Numbers. Numerals

0 zero	ज़ीरो	zīro
1 one	एक	ek
2 two	दो	do
3 three	तीन	tīn
4 four	चार	chār

5 five	पाँच	pānch
6 six	छह	chhah
7 seven	सात	sāt
8 eight	आठ	āth
9 nine	नौ	nau
10 ten	दस	das

11 eleven	ग्यारह	gyārah
12 twelve	बारह	bārah
13 thirteen	तेरह	terah
14 fourteen	चौदह	chaudah
15 fifteen	पन्द्रह	pandrah

16 sixteen	सोलह	solah
17 seventeen	सत्रह	satrah
18 eighteen	अठारह	athārah
19 nineteen	उन्नीस	unnīs

20 twenty	बीस	bīs
30 thirty	तीस	tīs
40 forty	चालीस	chālīs
50 fifty	पचास	pachās

60 sixty	साठ	sāth
70 seventy	सत्तर	sattar
80 eighty	अस्सी	assī
90 ninety	नब्बे	nabbe
100 one hundred	सौ	sau

200 two hundred	दो सौ	do sau
300 three hundred	तीन सौ	tīn sau
400 four hundred	चार सौ	chār sau
500 five hundred	पाँच सौ	pānch sau
600 six hundred	छह सौ	chhah sau
700 seven hundred	सात सो	sāt so
800 eight hundred	आठ सौ	āth sau
900 nine hundred	नौ सौ	nau sau
1000 one thousand	एक हज़ार	ek hazār
10000 ten thousand	दस हज़ार	das hazār
one hundred thousand	एक लाख	ek lākh
million	दस लाख (m)	das lākh
billion	अरब (m)	arab

3. Humans. Family

man (adult male)	आदमी (m)	ādamī
young man	युवक (m)	yuvak
woman	औरत (f)	aurat
girl (young woman)	लड़की (f)	larakī
old man	बूढ़ा आदमी (m)	būrha ādamī
old woman	बूढ़ी औरत (f)	būrhī aurat
mother	माँ (f)	mān
father	पिता (m)	pita
son	बेटा (m)	beta
daughter	बेटी (f)	betī
brother	भाई (m)	bhaī
sister	बहन (f)	bahan
parents	माँ-बाप (m pl)	mān-bāp
child	बच्चा (m)	bachcha
children	बच्चे (m pl)	bachche
stepmother	सौतेली माँ (f)	sautelī mān
stepfather	सौतेले पिता (m)	sautele pita
grandmother	दादी (f)	dādī
grandfather	दादा (m)	dāda
grandson	पोता (m)	pota
granddaughter	पोती (f)	potī
grandchildren	पोते (m)	pote
uncle	चाचा (m)	chācha
aunt	चाची (f)	chāchī
nephew	भतीजा (m)	bhatīja
niece	भतीजी (f)	bhatījī
wife	पत्नी (f)	patnī

husband	पति (m)	pati
married (masc.)	शादीशुदा	shādīshuda
married (fem.)	शादीशुदा	shādīshuda
widow	विधवा (f)	vidhava
widower	विधुर (m)	vidhur

| name (first name) | पहला नाम (m) | pahala nām |
| surname (last name) | उपनाम (m) | upanām |

relative	रिश्तेदार (m)	rishtedār
friend (masc.)	दोस्त (m)	dost
friendship	दोस्ती (f)	dostī

partner	पार्टनर (m)	pārtanar
superior (n)	अधीक्षक (m)	adhīkshak
colleague	सहकर्मी (m)	sahakarmī
neighbors	पड़ोसी (m pl)	parosī

4. Human body

body	शरीर (m)	sharīr
heart	दिल (m)	dil
blood	खून (f)	khūn
brain	मास्तिष्क (m)	māstishk

bone	हड्डी (f)	haddī
spine (backbone)	रीढ़ की हड्डी	rīrh kī haddī
rib	पसली (f)	pasalī
lungs	फेफड़े (m pl)	fefare
skin	त्वचा (f)	tvacha

head	सिर (m)	sir
face	चेहरा (m)	chehara
nose	नाक (f)	nāk
forehead	माथा (m)	mātha
cheek	गाल (m)	gāl

mouth	मुँह (m)	munh
tongue	जीभ (m)	jībh
tooth	दाँत (f)	dānt
lips	होंठ (m)	honth
chin	ठोड़ी (f)	thorī

ear	कान (m)	kān
neck	गरदन (m)	garadan
eye	आँख (f)	ānkh
pupil	आँख की पुतली (f)	ānkh kī putalī
eyebrow	भौंह (f)	bhaunh
eyelash	बरौनी (f)	baraunī
hair	बाल (m pl)	bāl

hairstyle	हेयरस्टाइल (m)	heyarastail
mustache	मूँछे (f pl)	münchhen
beard	दाढ़ी (f)	dārhī
to have (a beard, etc.)	होना	hona
bald (adj)	गंजा	ganja

hand	हाथ (m)	hāth
arm	बाँह (m)	bānh
finger	उँगली (m)	ungalī
nail	नाखुन (m)	nākhūn
palm	हथेली (f)	hathelī

shoulder	कंधा (m)	kandha
leg	टाँग (f)	tāng
knee	घुटना (m)	ghutana
heel	एड़ी (f)	erī
back	पीठ (f)	pīth

5. Clothing. Personal accessories

clothes	कपड़े (m)	kapare
coat (overcoat)	ओवरकोट (m)	ovarakot
fur coat	फरकोट (m)	farakot
jacket (e.g., leather ~)	जैकेट (f)	jaiket
raincoat (trenchcoat, etc.)	बरसाती (f)	barasātī

shirt (button shirt)	कमीज़ (f)	kamīz
pants	पैंट (m)	paint
suit jacket	कोट (m)	kot
suit	सूट (m)	sūt

dress (frock)	फ्रॉक (f)	frok
skirt	स्कर्ट (f)	skart
T-shirt	टी-शर्ट (f)	tī-shart
bathrobe	बाथ रोब (m)	bāth rob
pajamas	पजामा (m)	pajāma
workwear	वर्दी (f)	vardī

underwear	अंगवस्त्र (m)	angavastr
socks	मोज़े (m pl)	moze
bra	ब्रा (f)	bra
pantyhose	टाइट्स (m pl)	taits
stockings (thigh highs)	स्टाकिंग (m pl)	stāking
bathing suit	स्विम सूट (m)	svim sūt

hat	टोपी (f)	topī
footwear	पनही (f)	panahī
boots (e.g., cowboy ~)	बूट (m pl)	būt
heel	एड़ी (f)	erī
shoestring	जूते का फ़ीता (m)	jūte ka fīta

shoe polish	बूट-पालिश (m)	būt-pālish
gloves	दस्ताने (m pl)	dastāne
mittens	दस्ताने (m pl)	dastāne
scarf (muffler)	मफ़लर (m)	mafalar
glasses (eyeglasses)	ऐनक (m pl)	ainak
umbrella	छतरी (f)	chhatarī
tie (necktie)	टाई (f)	taī
handkerchief	रुमाल (m)	rūmāl
comb	कंघा (m)	kangha
hairbrush	ब्रश (m)	brash
buckle	बकसुआ (m)	bakasua
belt	बेल्ट (m)	belt
purse	पर्स (m)	pars

6. House. Apartment

apartment	फ़्लैट (f)	flait
room	कमरा (m)	kamara
bedroom	सोने का कमरा (m)	sone ka kamara
dining room	खाने का कमरा (m)	khāne ka kamara
living room	बैठक (f)	baithak
study (home office)	घरेलू कार्यालय (m)	gharelū kāryālay
entry room	प्रवेश कक्ष (m)	pravesh kaksh
bathroom (room with a bath or shower)	स्नानघर (m)	snānaghar
half bath	शौचालय (m)	shauchālay
vacuum cleaner	वैक्युम क्लीनर (m)	vaikyum klīnar
mop	पोंछा (m)	ponchha
dust cloth	डस्टर (m)	dastar
short broom	झाड़ू (m)	jhārū
dustpan	कूड़ा उठाने का तसला (m)	kūra uthāne ka tasala
furniture	फ़र्निचर (m)	farnichar
table	मेज़ (f)	mez
chair	कुर्सी (f)	kursī
armchair	हत्थे वाली कुर्सी (f)	hatthe vālī kursī
mirror	आईना (m)	āīna
carpet	कालीन (m)	kālīn
fireplace	चिमनी (f)	chimanī
drapes	परदे (m pl)	parade
table lamp	मेज़ का लैम्प (m)	mez ka laimp
chandelier	झूमर (m)	jhūmar
kitchen	रसोईघर (m)	rasoīghar
gas stove (range)	गैस का चूल्हा (m)	gais ka chūlha

electric stove	बिजली का चूल्हा (m)	bijalī ka chūlha
microwave oven	माइक्रोवेव ओवन (m)	maikrovev ovan
refrigerator	फ्रिज (m)	frij
freezer	फ्रीजर (m)	frījar
dishwasher	डिशवॉशर (m)	dishavoshar
faucet	टोंटी (f)	tontī
meat grinder	कीमा बनाने की मशीन (f)	kīma banāne kī mashīn
juicer	जूसर (m)	jūsar
toaster	टोस्टर (m)	tostar
mixer	मिक्सर (m)	miksar
coffee machine	कॉफ़ी मशीन (f)	kofī mashīn
kettle	केतली (f)	ketalī
teapot	चायदानी (f)	chāyadānī
TV set	टीवी सेट (m)	tīvī set
VCR (video recorder)	वीडियो टेप रिकार्डर (m)	vīdiyo tep rikārdar
iron (e.g., steam ~)	इस्तरी (f)	istarī
telephone	टेलीफ़ोन (m)	telīfon

·

Made in the USA
Middletown, DE
07 January 2024

47401404R00051